# FINAL EXPENSE LESSONS

Don't Let the Green Grass Fool Ya

By:

## Steven H. Gifford

Edited By:

Haleigh Lindner

Formatted By:

Christina Hobbs

I0478743

Copyright © 2017

## www.eClick.Insure

## "Insured with a CLICK"

"When you learn to mow your own lawn- you'll save more time and headaches than paying someone else."

"Steven G."

eClick Lawn Care

Own Your Own Lawn Care – Franchise with eClick Today!

No, it's not a lawn care business.  It's just a saying. Lol.

eClick "Insured with a CLICK"

# www.eclick.Insure

# Table of Contents

Introduction ................................................................................2

1.  What is The Green Grass... ...........................................................5

2.  Why  you can't leave the yard ................................................. 10

3.  Who is "THEY" .......................................................................... 15

4.  What Grass is bad ..................................................................... 20

5.  Where is the Good Grass ........................................................ 25

6.  Can Your Client be Bad Grass ................................................ 30

7.  Can Agents be Bad Grass ....................................................... 35

8.  Mow Your Own Yard ................................................................ 40

9.  The Best Grass Mower in the business ................................. 45

10. Own Your Own Lawn Care Business ...................................... 50

# Introduction

Final Expense can be a dirty business if you work for the wrong person, manager, or company. Most new agents are sold on the "You can be just like me if you do what I say" sales pitch. What you don't know… there are so many factors that are against you from ever achieving the success of that person. In my first book, "Final Expense Boot Camp", I go over the first thing you need to know. Who is the person recruiting you? Are they 5 levels from the top or are they the top of the food chain. It's important to know because while they are eating steaks- you'll be feeding off the bottoms of the trash cans if you don't work for the right person. They'll steal your pay. They'll charge you double for leads. They'll never promote you. So in essence- you'll be a middle-class agent, working your ass off- to pay their bills and fulfil THEIR dreams. Not Yours! We've seen it and this book will save you from years of wasted time, commissions, and headache. We serve you all the above on a golden platter. Sit back, enjoy the read, and get prepared to learn the things they never thought would be exposed.

# Don't Let the Green Grass Fool Ya

Chapter 1.

## What is the Green Grass?

We had a song we sang in the Marines while running.  Motivational chants per se to keep you in rhythm and in step- so the person behind you wasn't running all up on your heels.  You could hear the perfect methodical cadence of the left foot hitting the pavement.  It was a pretty cool thing to witness when the perfect cadence was being called, and the Marines would respond by chanting loudly, and that rhythm on the deck was precision.  If you were the enemy and heard these Marines charging at you… the sound of the footsteps would be enough to scare the lights out of ya.   The chant would go something like this:

"Don't Let.... Don't let the green grass fool ya.. (Marines would repeat it back)

"Don't let it... Change your Mind

(Marines would chant: "Your Mind, Your Mind, Your Mind"

I said, "Don't Let... Don't let the green grass fool ya... Don't let it... Change your mind..."

What is the green grass you ask? It can be two things. The grass you are standing on and the grass they never want you to see (your competitors or perhaps a better way of doing things). What do I mean the grass you're standing on?

1. Where you work. If you are in the final expense department- your grass is the manager who is hiring you and the company who is paying you.

2. The Grass is also the things they tell you that seem to be so great that no one else can possibly duplicate or even beat. It's

impossible to succeed anywhere else because the system in which they have... is just the best.  We also call it Kool Aid (otherwise known as BS).

3. The Green Grass can be all those things the manager says that you can achieve if you follow A, B, C and don't mess up one bit or it's your fault you failed.

What is the Green Grass on the other side- that they never want you to explore? Greener pastures perhaps, the truth, and a better way of mowing your own lawn (taking care of your own business). We'll explore this in another chapter.  What I want you to know and understand is this:  Final Expense is a tough, dirty, down and out fight- pull hair, punch you in the face business.  If you work for the wrong people that is.  I've seen more thieves, cons, and crooks in this business than any other.  I've worked in the night club business, mortgage business, Marines, and a lot of others but wall street and the white-collar sector criminals- have nothing on some of the managers and companies I have seen in the last ten years. So ... I started my own. If you ever knew a Marine you'll know these truths to be real.

1. A Marine Never Cheats, Lies, or Steals
2. A Marine takes care of their own. We never leave anyone behind. We accomplish the mission and we reward those who helped us along the way. PERIOD.

Are we perfect? No! Do we make mistakes? Absolutely. We correct them and move on with integrity, honor, and courage to admit we were wrong. I've actually had managers in the past criticize myself and others for being a Marine. They tell others that we run a boot camp type environment and we don't know how to run things. Fast forward 7 years and I've owned a million-dollar night club, wrote 8 books (1 a best seller #1 for 52 weeks), and now own the #1 Final Expense Telesales company in the US. PERIOD! So, in a sense we all have Green Grass. At the end of the day you gotta figure out who's telling you A, B, C to better them or who's telling you the truth to help YOU- the agent- who is new and naive to the business.  I'll give you a hint.  You'll see comments on the reviews, your managers telling you Steven G. sucks, and he doesn't own anything.  That's the Kool-Aid they serve you to keep you on their team. Stop drinking it, and figure it out on your own.

# Don't Let the Green Grass Fool Ya

Chapter 2

## Why You Can't Leave the Yard

My brother owns the cutest dog.  Her name is Satie.
She can be a Satan at times, but she's pretty good
the majority of the times.  He has to keep her on the
leash in the yard or in her cage if he leaves the
house. Sometimes, he'll take her up to the office
and let her run the show for a few hours as well.
Why does she have to be on a leash, a chain, or in
her cage you might ask?  Well, like most curious
dogs who are new born or young, she wants to
explore the world.  She smells those flowers in the
neighbor's yard from a mile away.  She hears the
birds chirping in the trees across the way.  She

doesn't know the dangers of the highway that runs on front of their home and she would unknowingly run right into traffic. So, there are good and bad reasons she must be on the chain. The #1 reason... She cost 5G's and he doesn't want her running away, getting lost, or getting killed from semi rolling down 598.

I'm not comparing an agent to a dog but we can all relate to that love, time spent, and money exchanged to get our pets. You build a bond and love and you just can't let it go. Compare that to you and your manager. He or she hires you, spend a lot of time training you, spend some cash getting you going perhaps, and they want that return of investment. Yes, you are an investment. A good manager deserves an over-ride or a commission of what you sell because they are taking time to train you. They take a risk with you because should you fail or leave the company and your business fails or falls off the books- they must repay it. So, a good manager deserves what they get- let's make that clear. With a good manager, they will change your lives. You owe them something for doing this.  How much do you owe them?  That's where the grass gets shit colored and stained because some are just greedy.  We'll cover more of this as well.

Your manager or company's goal is to keep you as an agent if they can- or with the company.  If you're making them 500 bucks a week times 52 weeks- that's a lot of money.  Some companies make you buy THEIR LEADS for 40 bucks – so multiply the profit of leads times 20 a week times 52 weeks and you'll see a whole other side of the game.  Oh, you didn't know those leads only cost $12.50 of $15.00 versus the $38.00 they are charging you because you're broke or you just don't know.  This is more Kool-Aid they tell you.  Again, we'll go over this as well.

You can't have other contracts, you can't purchase other leads and you can't talk to other managers or agents about YOUR contract because it's a "ONE BIG SECERET".  "Hey Steve, if you discuss your contract with any other agent... We'll terminate you." The fear factor sale (or the take away sale).  They know you're broke, and they know they have you by the neck on every level – so they take advantage of you.

I've heard funeral homes raping the survivor when it comes to paying for caskets, vaults, etc.  These managers out there are 10 times worst.  It's amazing how much they are making and how hard they make you work to pay their jets, cars, and homes off for them.  I hear some say, "I've been so fortunate in life and bla bla bla.. but they can't give a $30-dollar lead credit to a starving agent who showed up to a house where 5 other agents had been last week.  They sold the lead to 5 of the same agents in your area to make 150 bucks off that one lead.  Then they'll tell you it's your fault for not closing- or upselling the policy. Lol.  Kool- aid. You gotta stop drinking it.

## Chapter 3.

## Who is THEY?

They are the ones that are giving the Final Expense industry a bad rep.  Some of the companies do an excellent job while others run their MLM or Pyramids schemes so close to being illegal it's amazing they aren't shut down. I can't mention exact names but there are real insurance companies out there who do their best to do right with their clients and agents. The THEY in this chapter are those who are direct to or even have their own Final Expense Insurance companies.  There are also bad Regional Directors, managers, and agents who you need to avoid at all costs. How do you tell the difference?

1. An actual insurance company carries the paper for your client's policy.  They usually

pay you direct: Daily, weekly, over-rides, and residuals.  There are only two companies I know of that deal only with Final Expense but advertise they are an Insurance Company.  The only bad thing I learned from them- they make you BUY their leads at an up-charged price.  If you are working for an insurance company who makes you buy their $40.00 leads, while they are 2-3-4- months old... RUN!

2. An insurance agency is run buy someone who has been with the company and recruits agents. They have their own agency- but they still report to the company holding the paper.  If you work for an agency who pays you direct and it's not coming from the insurance company...RUN!  They are stealing your commissions and residuals. Promise ya!

3. Regional Director/ Regional Vice President/ Managing General Agent (MGA) these people are the ones making you buy

the leads, and keeping you on a 70-80 percent contract and trying to motivate you to hit 20k a month to fill their pockets. Some of them make a profit off the leads they buy from the company and re-sell them to you.  You'll never know how much they pay for them but I can tell you that we get the same lead or better for 1/3 of the price.  So, stop drinking their Kool-Aid. Do your homework.  Go outside your yard and learn.

Here are some things to look for when you are looking for THEY:

1. If they are driving an Escalade- You'll never get there. Why? Because there spread is so high- and they're not going to give it up.
2. If they are show boating their homes, cars, planes, watches, vacations- RUN!  You can't get there on your contract.
3. Do they make you buy THEIR LEADS?

4. Do they make you only work for them? You can't work for another company?

5. Are their leads over $20 bucks?

6. Are you seeing a lot of other agents have been to the same house- or called the same lead you have?  It happens occasionally but if you see this on every lead order- RUN!

7. Does your Manager pay you with cash on Friday? RUN. He's robbing you blind.

8. Does the Insurance Company- not an agency but a real insurance company- SALE LEADS—RUN.  They're in the lead business- not the taking care of agent's business.

9. Are you allowed to FINANACE their leads--- RUN.  They are charging you so much more because they know you can't afford to buy them on your own.

10.    Does your manager or company bad mouth others all the time- RUN! They are

only trying to keep you – because they know what they are about to lose.

11.     Do you hear that other agents have left- have never made it in the business? RUN!  We all leave – sometimes we leave because it's better.  We want to be where they are- and we're smart enough to see that we can't reach a 120% contract when you're on 80% and 5 managers ahead of you.  There's no way. You're stuck as an agent and you'll never be able to hire agents on 70% and keep them with $40.00 leads.  No way!

12.     Free leads- Make sure they will guarantee X amount in your area- and get it in writing. We worked for a company who said FREE leads and they wanted us to run 3-4-5- hours away to clean up leads in areas other agents quit on them. Sometimes, those leads were 6 months old but if you have no leads in your area- what are you going to do. It's a trap.  Free leads

aren't free- you pay for them.  That's another book.

13.     If you've been hitting good numbers and you're on a low contract and have to beg for a 5% bump- 1-2 years later- you're still on the same contract… RUN!  You deserve more. PERIOD!

Be smart, and just use your gut. If you can't trust the person, and you can't talk to them every day 2-3-4 times- leave.  There are so many other companies who will welcome you.

# Chapter 4.

## What Grass is Bad?

There is bad grass everywhere.  Does it just have to be the boss or the company you work for?  No!  Bad Grass can be the agent, the client, the lead company, and those who are recruiting you. You must be open-eyed and smart in this business.  It's a business.

Agents can be bad grass. So, if you're a manager you can't fall in love with your agents. You can't give them anything unless they earn it.  Why?  Because you earned yours. There is a reason why 80% of the agents leave a company and seek employment elsewhere. There is also that 10% who leave – whom you should have taken care of because you lost more than you ever gained by not giving them that 5%. We left a company – after hitting 236k in one month. That's 20k a month commission we were making. We left because they lied to us and were too greedy to give us the 5% they promised. I never saw 3 men dance around like cowards more than that day. If you live in Ohio, Florida you'll know who they are. One of the top Groups for the top company in final expense field sales. They have stolen more from agents and families than you could imagine. They lost more than they will ever know as well.

Clients? Can they be Bad Grass? Heck ya they can! They'll lie to you on every phone call, stand you up on the 2nd, 3rd, 4th appointment. They'll tell you they want the policy and you'll drive 2 hours- sign them up and the following month they cancelled. Most clients we deal with really want what we offer. We fill the need they have and help their families in the worst times of their lives. However, don't think they won't tell you what you want to get you out of the house or off the phones.  Don't fall in love with an application because it may not fund, and it will probably cancel.  How do you keep it from hurting you? You keep writing GOOD BUSINESS. If you're the agent writing 1-2 policies a month to get by and a policy doesn't fund like you planned- that's your fault for falling in love with it. You should have had 10 policies in the pipeline expecting some of it not to go through.  Don't fall in love with your clients or their policies. Get as many in as you can for YOUR LAWN, your family, and your business.

Those companies who are recruiting you… Can they be BAD GRASS?  Damn right!  These people will tell you anything to get you on their team.  I've been flown around the world, recruited by the best, dinners at the 5 star restaurants, and red carpet laid out beneath my feet.  They make you feel like you're a god send, the best in the world, and with their system- you can rule the world.  Wait till a week later when the newness wears off.  You're one of 100 or 1000 apples in a tree and they couldn't care about you or your agents. You start from the bottom again, and you're a nobody. You think, wow! How could they recruit me so hard, and the next week after I sign my contract, bring over 40 agents, and commit to their perfect system ignore my calls? I was talking to the President at dinner, the CEO and owner wanted to work out with me at the gym, they cared about me being a Marine and had my favorite Bible Verse on the receptionist desk as they lead me there- so blatantly planned it was almost sickening. I mean, buyer beware- the green grass isn't always greener. Sometimes it is best to stay where you're at. Think for yourself and smell the grass on your own. You'll know in time. My favorite sales pitch—You have to decide right now – or that top contract won't be available to you. Um... RUN!

Last but not least- the lead companies. You have to be very careful when you buy leads.

Most are reselling to 3-4-5 other agents.  You'll call the client and they have no idea who or why you are calling them.  You'll show up to a house that's boarded up, no one answers, or they swear to God that they never sent the card in.  My favorite is when you were just at a house that had seen one of you co-agents the week prior.  You're running the leads of your new agent and end up to Ms. Jones' house whom you just saw the week prior.  So that company-sold that lead 4 times.  They made 200 bucks on one lead and are a million-dollar company.  How sad is that?   You have to resell your own leads to other agents to pay your bills.  If you get a string of clients who other agents you know just say… RUN.  There isn't a perfect lead, company, manager, or even agents.  However, if they are blatantly lying to you to put food on their tables… What would they do when you build an empire with them.  They get worst and we've seen it. You won't get that raise, they'll push the 6 months old leads on you and your agents. Why? Because the more you have vested in their company- the more agents you have in their system- the harder it is for you to leave and start over. You are trapped. So, get our when you see any sign of blatant lies, bad leads and or any issues with pay. RUN!

## Chapter 5.

## Where is the Green Grass?

I go over this in my first book (#1 on Amazon for 52 weeks straight) "Final Expense Boot Camp". You must know the person and company you are going to work with.  Do your homework.  Is that person straight to the company?  Or are they 5-6- levels down?  Every level down the chain-link you are- is about 10% of your pay that you give up.  It's ok to be 2-3 levels down if the person who is hiring you has a top contract per se. If they are on a 90% contract offering you 75%- your top contract that you will ever get is 80%.  You can't build an agency like the Regional Director has on an 80% contract.  No Way.  So, you and the 100 other agents who they lied to, sold, and conned to get onboard are going to waste 1-2-3 years of your life but that's ok- because they'll make 100k on you during that time. When you leave, they'll steal your agents, your residuals, and tell everyone that you won't make it with any other company. So, make sure you're on a good contract for a new agent. Make sure you can advance in your career. Ask them what your top contract will be in 1-2-5 years. If they stumble around and dance around the question, RUN!

Does the company or agency have a good lead source for you to use? Are they leads a fair price? Are they EXCLUSIVE to YOU? A fair lead these days is around $15.00 bucks. Anything less, they are reselling them or getting them from the internet- resold and selling to you. Those leads have as much of a chance of closing than you do being a millionaire on a 75% contract. I don't know of any.

Does the company have a training program? Some companies offer a training class, ride along, and or hands on training.  Some offer online, 24/7 training where you can go at your own speed- take it over if you need to.  Some can do screen shares and weekly online meetings if you are spread out from your main company.  Some offer you ZERO. Say, good luck to you. RUN!  Look for a good training program and someone who will spend time with you one on one.  If they agree to do that- that's a great start. If they can't seem to answer your calls the first week… RUN!

Can you advance in that company?  Is it spelled out on paper how far you can go.  Can you own a piece of the company, or own your own franchise even?  Do they make it mandatory to wait 6-12 months to be a manager, 2 years to have your own agency, 3 years to be an RVP?  Is this fair to an agent with 10 years of experience who is starting over because he or she moved- or they want to do phone sales versus field? No!  Find a company you don't have to start over with per se, and work your butt off to prove yourself worthy of the contract they give you.

Look at the company's website, or the agencies website, or the person recruiting you- does he or she have their name on the site, or name on the manager's board, leaders board, office location board?  Are they someone in the company?  If their website looks like 1990 which I will say a lot of companies have copied our site at www.eclick.insure .  5 years ago- these managers and agencies didn't have websites. We have changed the way a lot of them do things and you'll see a lot of their sites look like ours.  Why?  Because they know what or who the best was- so they followed the leader.  It's ok- we're always implementing new and more technical ways to better the industry and we love when others copy us- that means we're doing things right.

Can you talk to the person who is recruiting you 3-4-5 times a day- for the next 6 months? That's how much effort it's going to take to get you going if you are new.  If you aren't new- are you willing to still put your pride to the side and listen to someone who knows what works?  I see it all the time- agents saying I was the best at this or that, talk for an hour about how great they are, and promise you that they'll be #1 in your company the first month.  They last about a week.  Get rid of the them… RUN!  If you can find the good lead, good training, and good contract that allows you to advance to the top- lock on to that company and give it your all. That's all you can do.  Do your homework.

# Don't Let the Green Grass Fool Ya

## Chapter 6

## Can Your Client be Bad Grass?

How do you know when your client is lying to you?  As soon as they open their mouths!  I heard this years ago, and it took me awhile to actually understand it.  You can ask a client when you get in their home if they experienced a funeral lately – is that why they sent the card in, or wanted information about final expense?  They'll say Nope.  You'll go on for 10 minutes, re-telling that script your manager had you memorise per every word.   You'll tell them the average funeral is about 12-15k – does that sound about right to you Mr. Jones?  Oh, ya – I just buried my mom.  Her funeral was $13,500.45.  What the heck?  They just told you they hadn't experienced a funeral and now… THEIR MOM JUST DIED?  Why did they open up to you suddenly?

You built re-port. They know you're there to help them.  It's amazing how things change when they know you're not a telemarketer and they build a little trust with ya.  A client can have a difficult day.   Their dog just died, kids are sick, husband is a drunk, and they just walked in the door with 3 bags of groceries and dinner needs cooked before the kids must go to basketball practice.  They've had 100 agents who showed up to their door- especially with the company I talked about earlier lol.  They get calls from 100 people who can't speak English- asking if they need a dental plan, car washed, or someone to make a web site for them for free.  Of course, they're going to tell you NO, they're not interested.  However, once you build that trust up- they'll eat from your hands.

Why else can they be bad grass?  Some clients can't afford a policy but they have one thing we all have in us-  PRIDE. They don't want to tell you that they are broke on the 5th of the month and their SSI doesn't hit for another 25 days. So, they tell you to come back, or they want to think about it, or worst- they actually sign up knowing the money isn't in the bank.  They just want you out of their home- so they can watch the Wheel of Fortune, Judge Judy, or the Price is Right from 1999 with Bob Barker. Lol.

Sometimes the Bad Grass isn't the actual client- it's the policy they take (the policy you made them take).  What?  You mean that $134.00 policy I sold them wasn't helping them out?  I need to pay rent so I had to convince them the 50k plan was best for them- even knowing they had to wait till the first of next month to make a payment and it's the 7th of this month and they are broke!!  Make sense?  That's bad business- bad grass and it's not going to grow to long because they can't afford it.  You as the professional need to write good business for the client- not for YOUR BILLS.  You do what's right for the client and it'll come back 10 times.  I have a client in Oregon that I treated right 2 years ago. I've sold over 30 policies to her and her family. I've made over 20k on 1 client – by being nice.  She called me tonight actually, and I signed her son up for a policy. I could have made it 400k and made 1500 bucks, but I made it 50k and said once you make a few a payments, I'll get you another one.  He loved the idea.  Now he's referring me to his wife's parents and they each want a policy.  So, it's going to keep paying for a while longer.  Write good business, take care of your clients and your lawn will grow greener much longer than you ever thought.

Chapter 7.

## Can Agents Be Bad Grass?

I mentioned earlier that there is a reason an agent is 55 years old and looking for a new career with another company- because his last company didn't train him right, the leads sucked, and his manager was a lunatic Marine who smoked a pack a day. Lol.  Said agent talked your ear off for an hour in the interview about how he was the #1 salesmen with Kirby Vacuums in 1985.  He couldn't shut up long enough for you to get a word in and pulled his wallet out showing you his 9 kids and 34 grand kids- all with the letter J as the first letter in their name.  I mean what a better agent to hire right? RUN!  I've literally walked out of interviews, told them to walk out, or just laughed while checking emails for an hour and played the game with them.

You must hire GOOD AGENTS.  I'm not going to give all my secrets away but don't waste your time on Bad Grass- agents who think they know it all or can be #1 in a week.  Let them go.

If you have an agent who will work their asses off and show it- yet don't have a lot of knowledge- that's the agent I'll work with.  I can train you in final expense. I cannot train you how to work and provide for your family.  Make sense?

If you have an agent who doesn't call you the first week, they are doing things there way, and re-designed the script on day one.  RUN!  Get rid of them. You don't need someone who wants to build their own final expense company with no experience.  I was that agent at first but I listened, learned and proved myself.  I did learn new things that a company I was with-didn't teach and they refused to believe it worked.  Fast forward 7 years- they're all using it.  So, it goes both ways.

If you have an agent who has friends and family he can count on to build his business with policies they are going to buy… RUN!  If they can't buy into the system you're running- or at least try it out first- don't waste your time on them.  If they're broke and willing to call from a phone book 12 hours a day till they get money to buy leads.  That's the agent I'm hiring all day long.

The only questions I want to hear from an agent are:

1. What time do the lights go off?  I want to work late.
2. Can you shut the alarm off for me- I don't want it going off at midnight when I am working? This happened to me once.

3. How many leads can I order today- and can I order more on Wednesday when I kill it Monday and Tuesday?

4. Can I work Weekends- Great!

5. Boss, get out of here- I'm working late tonight to hit my goal this week. I'm staying with that agent until he's done. Lol.

6. Hey boss, can I start today? I can just watch you make some calls- We'll get the contracts out tomorrow.

7. You mind if I get some older leads and hire my wife to call them for me so we can double our efforts?

8. What's the most someone has sold in a day? How can I do what they did?

9. I suck at sales but I'll work my ass off.

10. You got a charger- My phone's dead from calling so many people. Lol.

When you find a GOOD AGENT- take care of them. They are hard to come by. I've been that agent- and I've seen a few. I've always taken care of those who work hard.  They don't have to ask for a raise- we give it to them.  We bend over backwards for those who bend over backwards for our company.  It's part of the Marine Motto-  Accomplish the mission and Troop welfare- take care of your Marines. Some of the managers I have worked under- need a lesson on how to manage people.  We earned what we got. Nothing was handed to us.

# Don't Let the Green Grass Fool Ya

Chapter 8.

## Mow Your Own Lawn

One of the four Leadership Principles for the Marines is: Seek Self Improvement- always look to better yourself and your Marines.  I have found this principle a leading factor in everything I have done in every career I have endeavoured.  I've started at the bottom of the food chain in the nigh club business, mortgage business, and now the final expense industry. In each field, I have excelled and eventually owned a business in each field mentioned above.  The night club made a million our first year.  The Mortgage Business was thriving until the collapse that we all were effected by. Now, I own the #1 Final Expense Telesales company in the US.  I don't tell you this to brag, but to show you that an average kid in high school, went into the Marines, and did whatever he had to do to lead Marines.  I did what I had to do to be #1 at just about everything I have done since. Why? There are probably a million reasons but the one that sticks out to me the most is PRIDE.  You have to have pride in what you do- even when no one else is watching.  I was the type of person that was going to the library to study till it closed, hitting the gym at 0200 in the am so I could be the strongest Marine. I would google Mortgage Leads online all weekend long and find out if I could create a better one.  I would study Mortgage Lingo- because I has no idea what I was doing. I learned a lot of it on my own.   I memorized the script given to me when I started as an agent in Final Expense. My first day in the field I sold six policies. I had to. I was broke!  I was embarrassed and I wanted to be #1 again.

You have to put the time into YOU, YOUR BUSINESS, and YOUR SUCCESS.  If you give 100% at anything you do in life- You'll be successful.  We can find a million reasons why something isn't perfect, or it doesn't work for me, or why others are doing better.   When you stop playing in others GRASS and focus on YOURS-  No one can stop you. PERIOD!

Who cares if Jen is #1 in the office or John hit 20k last month.  Does it put food on your table? You think they were given the GOOD leads, and you're on the HATE list of the office so you get the shit leads.  You think that because you were #1 at the gold pro shop you worked at – that you have to be #1 at phone sales.  That could be the furthest from the truth.  You have to be open minded, coachable and willing to work as hard as we did to learn the business.  You have to put the time in- just like we did to get better. You have to go over your scripts, objections, and products over and over until you are the subject matter expert of final expense.  When you do that- You'll be a very rich person.

You can literally change your life when you change your thinking. When you're out smoking with Harry and Shelly- they are complaining how bad those leads suck. You noticed they did the best presentation, gave three quotes, the client picked one and then they pissed their pants. They asked for the check immediately, they told them that they'd call them back tomorrow just to make sure they were ok with their decision. They did everything they weren't supposed to do to close that deal but those leads suck. Lol.

My favorite is the agent who you haven't heard from in 2 weeks tell you they called their leads and no one was home or no one wanted to talk to them. They already had insurance and no one in Michigan wanted final expense. I go and call the leads with them and sell 3 apps the first 3 calls I make on their list. That agent wasn't working and made every excuse in the world on why he couldn't close a deal- and it was not his fault because he was the best at the Kirby Sales.

You have to ignore the agents who are brining YOU DOWN.  Who cares if they can't close a fridge door.  Who cares if they can't afford $12.50 cent leads.  They are broke because they've always blamed the system or someone else.  They hung around the alley's in school smoking weed while we were inside learning how to read, write and add.  Their mom and dad gave them everything in life while some of us went off and earned it via the Marines, College, or Sports.  Some of us had to work for our food and we never wanted our kids to go through that experience.  Some of us were #1 in life and love the feeling of being accomplished.  Some of us lead while others watch and complain to other agents about how we get all the good leads and calls that come in.

You must put all that Green Grass Nonsense to the side and just focus on YOU.  Study your ass off, go the extra mile, ask for help, and seek self-improvement. Don't worry about how much Arron did, or where the others are going for lunch. When they leave, the office is quite which means you can focus even more. When they leave at 6PM to go to the gym- you stay and hit those 1-2 extra sales. 1 sale a night two nights out of the week is an extra 2000.00 in your pocket every month. That's 24k a year folks. Simply working an extra 1-2 hours a night- two days a week while others wanted to get home to do nothing. Take a morning off, take a break in the afternoon- hit the gym, take your wife to dinner. Than you go back home- or you're in your office and make 10 more calls. You'll get that sale and then you can take a long weekend with your wife and be able to afford her wishes and dreams. So many people look at the NOW versus the 6-12-month goal. I did too! I wasn't perfect but it hit me. If I work 2 times harder now, I won't have to work 2 times longer to hit my dreams.

Stay in YOUR YARD.  Focus on YOUR DREAMS.  Never let anyone steal your passion or your willing to be #1.  If you do that- you will succeed no matter which company you are with. Perhaps one day you'll own the next eClick Franchise.  We'll talk about that next.  Stay the course and set goals. Do whatever it takes to hit those goals and then set another one.  Never get complacent on where you are and what you are doing.

# Don't Let the Green Grass Fool Ya

Chapter 9

## The Best Mower in the Business

With so many companies out there today a new agent must be lost when it comes to knowing who is the best. I mean, there are literally hundreds of companies, thousands of Kool-Aid bread leaders, con artist managers and agents who will do anything to get a sale. What makes eClick the best in Telesales? We were agents at one time. We understand the trials and obstacles you are about to embark upon- even new managers. I have always said to myself that if I can't find the right product or company to do things RIGHT.. I'll build it myself. It took me 10 years to get to where I am at. I not only own eClick "Insured with a CLICK" but an online final expense planning site called ePlot. (www.ePlot.us)

ePlot was concepted on the idea of a soldier being deployed and having to leave a last note to his loved ones with his buddy- in case he didn't make it back home. We said there has to be a better way to leave a note, message, video, legacy, and final wish- so that others could know who you were and see your contributions that you made while you were alive. Maybe you wanted to wish your son a happy birthday. Perhaps you wanted to leave a video to be played at your daughter's wedding. ePlot is our planning portion of eClick. We allow you the agent to give it to YOUR CLIENTS for free.

No other Telesales Company can offer the product that we do- because we own it. By giving the ePlot to your clients for free- we feel that it gives them something they can touch or feel. It cements their plans and the policy attached to it. For those clients who are older and not computer savvy we suggest you purchase a few of our final expense planning guides that allows them to plan their wishes with a pen.  By giving them that planner- you can also put your card in it, and referral page, and a welcome letter.  Call them up in a few days and make sure they received the package and ask for some referrals.  The planner is 100 pages but a lot of it is where they write in it if they want. It's an easy read for them. It also explains how to set up their online "ePlot" or legacy page for free.  A simple $5.00 gift to them will keep your business on the books, get you referrals, and allow your client to pre- plan their final wishes online or via the planner. This will allow their family to know exactly what they want done and reduce arguments at that time.

ePlot also had "Guardians" who can make the final calls- notifying their friends and loved ones of their passing.  This eliminates their loved ones from telling the horrific details of the death over and over reducing a little bit of the pain left from the death of their loved ones.

ePlot has partnered with a company off shore that produces a very high quality lead at a very fair price.  We have appointment leads, avatar leads and live transfers that range from $12.50 to $19.99 for live transfers.  We don't own the company but they believe in us and are growing with us nationwide.  If I want them to change a word in the script they change it.  If I feel their agents pushed too hard on a call- they'll credit the lead.  The leads are 100% exclusive and they want you to succeed because they know you'll order more- which keeps them in business.  We make .50 cents on a lead and this is the most we will make because we feel that keeping lead cost down allows you the agent to purchase more.  If you are buying more leads- you are writing more business.  This puts money in all party's pockets.  Its only makes sense.  Why would you charge 800 bucks for 20 leads and make an agent starve, suffer, or even quit because they couldn't get a sale?

Our philosophy is 360 degrees different. If we give you the right contract – which we will go over next, a great lead, and the tools to make you successful- how can you not succeed.  We want you motivated to get up and work. We want you to enjoy your life and the company you work with.  We don't push you to work every day 18 hours a day so you can hit our goals.  You'll never see us post that we need to hit 500k or we had a record month of 1.2 million. Who cares. It doesn't help you out.  We want you to be happy, hit your goals, and put food on your families table.  If you have a sense of ownership, a pride of who you work with, and an opportunity to become a partner with us and share in the company's success—that is how we operate.  I mentioned before, that the Marine Motto is to accomplish the mission and then to take care of those Marines in their charge. It is the back bone of what we have built.  A lot of companies promise you that the agents come first.  We show it to you right off the back.

eCick has dominated the final expense telesales side of the house.  We also have the same opportunity with field agents.  We can get the same lead within an hour of a big city. If you're around Columbus, Dallas, Houston, Chicago, etc. – we can get you the same quality leads.  Maybe you don't like telesales but you like a top contract or a lead that hasn't been sold to 5 agents for 40 bucks.  Maybe you like the opportunity to own your own franchise.  We give you all the opportunity to choose the level that you want to come on at.  Again, if we allow you to have that sense of ownership and or the ability to own your own franchise – we feel you'll work harder to help us build our brand and continue leading the way in Telesales.

For more information on why eClick- you can visit us online and click on the WHY ECLICK tab at the top.  Make sure you visit the ePlot site as well. Watch the video on the homepage and eClick "Insured with a CLICK"   www.eClick.Insure

you'll see exactly what we give you and your
clients for free.

# Don't Let the Green Grass Fool Ya

## Chapter 10.

# Own Your Own Lawn Care Franchise

In the Marine Corps, you are usually assigned to a unit for 1 or 3 years.  The reason it to allow you to build trust and respect for those Marines you are going to lead into battle.  When you show up to a new unit you sit back and observe, go with the flow per se and gradually earn your Marines trust.  If you come in as the Drill Instructor who is demanding everyone change to his ways or the highway- it's not going to go over to well.  On the other hand- if you're a Sergeant at one unit and get transferred to another- you don't have to start all over as a Private.  You earned your rank and respect while being promoted to your rank. You earned it and everyone knows what you had to do to get it. It's not handed out per se. We use this approach at eClick.

We don't make you start over as an agent if you're a proven leader in the game. Why would we? We feel that if you are trying to progress- perhaps you need a higher contract, or you want to do phone sales, or you need a cheaper lead, perhaps you're stuck at the level you're at and won't ever be able to have your own agency- we get it.

We give you the choice to come on at the level you're comfortable at- as well as an opportunity to own your own eClick Franchise. Again, we want you to have ownership in what you do, along with the pride of owning your own business. We want to give you the tools right off the back that will allow you to run your shop as you see fit. If you want to come on as an agent- that's fine too. Do you have to have 100 agents to come on as a franchise? No! Most start with themselves to get the highest contract possible, the free website which allows all recruits to go to you, and the partnership with eClick that will last a long time.  Whatever level you are comfortable with... You pick it.  We've had agents come on, learn the system and within a month decide they want to go all in and become a Franchisee.  We've had agents come on straight as a Franchisee because they wanted the best – right off the back.  They wanted to own their own franchise and be able to recruit all the agents in their states.

eClick has a duplicable system that hires, contracts, and trains your agents 24/7 online and monthly classes that anyone can attend. You just have to manage them.  We have the perfect system to hire, train and work from anywhere in the US.  You could be in Florida and recruiting in California.  You can work anywhere in the world as well.  No one will know.   We wrote another book called "Franchising Final Expense" and it goes into detail on why this program is dominating the industry.  Learn how to make 100-200k a month within 6 months of coming on board.  You can go to www.amazon.com  and search Final Expense. You'll see 6-7 books that we have written.  Each detailing an aspect that is very important in this business.

We wish you the best- no matter who you want to work for.  Focus on YOU and YOUR LAWN and it'll grow just fine.  We appreciate you taking the time to read this book.

Steven G.

# Semper Fidelis!

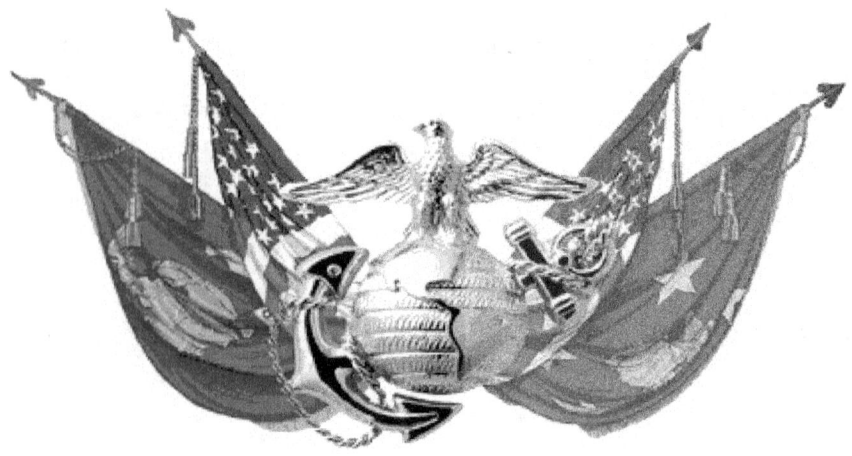

Any Media or Speaking Requests, please email:

TeamOne@eClick.Insure

# Don't Let the Green Grass Fool Ya

**Hiring Our- Heroes World Wide- Work from home**

## www.eClick.Insure